# 2066 AND ALL THAT

# 2066

## AND ALL THAT

Ben Yarde-Buller &

Sophie Duncan

First published in 2007 by
Old Street Publishing Ltd, 28-32 Bowling Green Lane,
London EC1R 0BJ, UK
www.oldstreetpublishing.co.uk

ISBN-13: 978-1-905847-29-7

10 9 8 7 6 5 4 3 2 1

## DEDICATION

We would like to dedicate this book to our children Joe and Rebecca, who are both Very Good Things even though from time to time they cause Waves of Exhaustion, Panic, Runny Noses etc; and to Alexandra Yarde-Buller, without whom neither this book nor the children would exist.

# CONTENTS

## Before Word

Not long after the Peace to end Peace had been signed in the Hall of Mirrors, the two Top Historians[*] of the time carelessly wrote in their Masterpiece[†] that 'America was thus Top Nation, and History came to a .' This was not a full sentence and also incorrectly punctured, and must have been due either to Reaching the Present or Running Out Of Ink, both of which are known to cause the End of History.

However, the Present Present is different from the Past Present (and hopefully has nothing to do with the Future Perfect). It is thus invariably time for a new History Book, in which the Past Simple is changed into the Past Historic: a very different and altogether less serious matter.

## Word

America is still Top Nation today, and therefore must be mentioned at indecent intervals in all History Books, including this one. However, it should be argued whenever possible that

---

[*] W.C. Sellar and R.J. Yeatman
[†] *1066 and all that*, London: Methuen, 1930

British people are rather superior. For example, ninety-three percent of Americans are born without a sense of humour owing to their obese diet of burgers and pancakes for breakfast, and are vulgar, naïve, unsofisticated etc.

## AFTER WORD

The Author reserves the unequivocal right of all Historians to mislead, misinterpret, misspell and (in the case of jokes) misfire, and would fully expect the Reader to do the same, given the opportunity.

## Chapter 1

# THE BIRTH OF THE MODERN ERA

T HE EXACT TIME and date of the Birth of the Modern Era is debatable (especially by Top Historians), and thus, along with other times and dates, *not memorable*. However, there is a bored consensus that it took place soon after the Death of Innocence in some fields near Flanders.

*A Bored Consensus*

## The Essential Futility of Modern Life

Before the Death of Innocence in Flanders, British people had an *Imperial Mentality*. This meant that they enjoyed:

- Humming *Cool Britannia*
- Ruling the Waves
- Helping Natives to Help Themselves
- Helping Themselves to Natives

However, once the War had shown them the Essential Futility of Modern Life (c.f. *The Waist Line*, by T.S. Eliot), they immediately stopped doing all these things and began to Debunk them instead.[*]

The Top Debunker was the scabrous Ineffectual Lytton Scratchy, whose book *Imminent Victorians* was an Irrelevant (but sensationally Witty) Satire on the Establishment.[†] In *Imminent Victorians* Scratchy wittily showed quite how Essentially Futile everything was, except slim volumes filled with elegant prose. (These were futile, but essential.)

Lytton Scratchy was quite Imminent himself, being a member of the highly Ineffectual Bloomsbury Group, who were

---

[*] This occurred on a Wednesday afternoon at half past four.

[†] Queen Victoria

all sensationally witty and irrelevant about everything, even important matters such as Life and Death. However, being rather elite, they did not speak to ordinary people and thus were unpopular with plumbers, cobblers, fish wives etc.

*The Scabrous Ineffectual Lytton Scratchy*

## Roaring - A Modern Pastime

The Death of Innocence together with the Flu Epidemic (excessively ironic as it killed even more people than the War to End Peace) soon started to cause a Great Depression.

English people in the Twenties tried to ward off the Depression by Roaring* at every opportunity, which was a memorable but noisy tactic.

The Bright Young Thingummyjigs Roared† more than anyone else, as they were easily bright enough to understand that the War had killed all their boyfriends.

*The Roaring Twenties*

However, the French and Germans also roared a lot, and even went so far as to change the name of a valley they jointly owned from the 'Rhine' to the 'Ruhr', which means 'Roar' in both languages.

---

* and sometimes Flapping
† and Flapped

## Modernists

All artists and writers of this period called themselves Modernists to show that they were not nearly as old-fashioned as their parents. Modernists spent all their time cultivating modernistic gardens, attitudes and especially hairstyles. When they were asked what they believed in they almost always just laughed carelessly and said 'Art for God's Sake!', thus proving beyond reasonable doubt that they were Bohemian as well as Modernist.

A group of six or more Modernists is called Modernism. More than twenty chatting all at once in a single room may be termed Modernity.

## The Rise of Women

One of the most Modern issues of all was the issue of whether women should be given a) the vote b) the franchise c) both or d) neither.

There was much opposition to a) based on several facts:

i) Women would vote hysterically, which would cause Scenes in polling booths and thus be a Bad Thing for the Nation.

*Hysterical Voting*

ii) Women would stop being innocent and/or charming.[*]

iii) Women would Rise, causing The Rise of Women and other grotesque consequences (such as Janet Street-Porter and/or Male Nurses[†]).

---

[*] and/or both
[†] and/or both

Others responded to these arguments, mostly with counter-arguments:

i) Even the Most Hysterical Woman* would vote for the same person as her husband.

ii) Women without the vote were not charming and innocent. Quite the reverse, they were Disenfranchised.

iii) Unlike the Rise of Unemployment and the Rise of Nastyism, the Rise of Women would be a Good Thing.

There was far less discussion about whether women should be given the franchise, as nobody really understood what it meant.

In the end, thanks to these counter-arguments (as well as the powerful lyrics of *The Suffragettes*), all Feminists over the age of 30 were given the vote. This was a Good Start, but still Unfair, as Hominists were allowed to vote at the age of 21.

Eventually, however, the law was changed to make Feminists and Hominists equal. From this time on *The Suffragettes* began to lose popularity, causing one prominent member of the band to throw herself in front of the King's Horse in despair.

_____

* Isadora Duncan

## Conclusion (Sententious)

The Rise of Women is one of the most significant rises of the Modernist Age and is to be sincerely welcomed.

Today it is literally impossible to imagine a world in which women felt so disenfranchised that they wished to be trampled by a horse. Such contemporary women as Posh Spice and Dame Edna would not dream of being trampled by a horse or indeed any other hoofed quadruped. However, it is incumbent on the Historian to try to understand the very different circumstances of those who lived in the past. After this, it is incumbent to laugh at how silly they were, and congratulate oneself on the Immense Strides that have been made since then.

## Modern Politics

Owing to the War to End Peace and the Death of Innocence, many people controversially began to see themselves as Lions led by Donkeys, instead of vice-versa as had always been the case in more old-fashioned times. An overwhelming majority thus voted for the Labour Party or the Liberals (Lions) instead of the Tories (mostly Donkeys). As a result, a Labour Prime Minister – Pansy Macdonald – suddenly found himself in an Office for the first time.

## The General Strike

During the War to End Peace, workers had been given stimulants by the Government to boost production. However this stopped after the Peace to end Peace, causing a Wave of Industrial Unrest.

Finally the Workers became so Unrestful that they called a General Strike. This was a terrible bother for the Government, as it caused the wheels of industry to grind to a halt.

*Starvation: A Victory for the Government*

The TUC (the largest factory in the country) gave out free cheese biscuits during the Strike, causing temporary relief. However the biscuits ran out after only eight days and the Workers began to starve: a Victory for the Government.

## Sort of Abroad: Ireland

At this time Ireland was still just a Colony located just off England, famous for Potato Famines and a Question.[*]

Soon after the War the British Prime Minister Lloyd-George finally decided to give an Answer to the Irish Question[†], as it had been causing him some Troubles (even though he was Welsh). However, Lloyd-George's answer[‡] did not satisfy the Irish, who would have preferred a Solution[§], and thus they continued to behave in a most Irregular manner.

## Definitely Abroad: Russia

A Russian Revolution took place some time during the War to End Peace, either in October or perhaps November. It began when a Pseudonym known as Linen steamed with consummate timing into the Capital on a train from Finland, executing the entire Tsar and all his family the moment he stepped out onto the platform. Linen thus firmly established that he was Ruthless and on no account a Trifle.

---

[*] The Irish Question

[†] No

[‡] No

[§] Yes

Linen soon proved his ruthlessness even more by killing Rasputin* with a hammer and sickle while he was out skating on the frozen wastes. Rasputin was a highly magnetic Holy Man and thus could transfix a minimum of ten aristocratic women (including the Tsarina herself) to the wall of a church merely by staring at them and tugging his beard.

*Rasputin Transfixing Russian Women*

There were two other memorable Revolutionaries apart from Linen: Trotsky and Stalin. Both were somewhat jealous of Linen's Pseudonym (Linen), which they wished they had

---

* arguably Russia's greatest love machine

thought of themselves. The trio were known as 'Bolshy Viks', because they rarely smiled.

After the Revolution Linen unruthlessly died after a series of ill-advised strokes. However, his memorable relics were preserved in a special Morseleum on Red Square.

*Linen's Morseleum*

Stalin and Trotsky then travelled to Mexico to have a lethal duel with an ice-pick (in order to decide who would replace Linen). Stalin won thanks to the unfair assistance of a secret agent.

The Historian should remember **at all times** that Russia is significantly more backward than the West, and therefore duels, ice-picks, ice-packs, hammers and sickles are only to be expected.

## The Feimar Republic: Not Very Interesting

The Feimar Republic was Germany's new name after the war, as it was considered a terrible *faux-pas* to utter the word Germany aloud. At first the Feimar Republic was rather stable and thus of no real interest except to obscure Historians. However, the situation began to improve due to the appearance of Adolf Hitler and his Nasti party.

The rise of the Nasti party was caused by these factors:

- The Wailure of the Weimar Republic, for highly complex, manifold and not very memorable reasons.
- The popularity of a new dance move called the goose-step, which was Hitler's brain-child.

*The Goose-Step*

- The Great Depression, which put the wind in Hitler's sails as everyone was sighing*.
- Sheer outrage that on 28 October 1929 half a frankfurter cost more than a million Marx. This day was immediately dubbed Black Monday, and all the Thugs in the country put on Black Shirts in celebration of it.
- Many German school children felt that the terms laid down by the Versailles Treaty were too long.

At this time Hitler was not yet a Dictator, as he kept being sent to prison for attempted Putsches†, which were illegal.

### Conclusion

Thus, in conclusion, was the Modern Era born.

---

* also due to their high level of Inflation
† tantrums

## End of Chapter Test

**You are advised NOT to answer questions b), d) or h)**

a) Which of the following contemporary females is least likely to be trampled\*: Marge Simpson, the Queen, Posh Spice, Dame Edna? Do not give reasons for your answer.

b) Give a pithy yet verbose summary of the main differences between Roaring and Flapping.

c) Disguise your lack of understanding of the principles of economics via a series of knowing allusions to the Gold Standard, Inflation, Exports, and the Balance of Trade.

d) With reference to primary sources, sketch first a Lion then a Donkey (or vice-versa). Which is which?

f) Outline Rasputin.

g) Is Life Essentially Futile? Answer from the point of view of either a Bright Young Thingummyjig or a Modernist.

h) Is this an Irish Question? If not, what is it?

---

\* by a horse or any other hoofed quadruped

## Chapter 2

# THE THIRTIES – A DREADFUL DECADE

THE THIRTIES WERE a Dreadful Decade during which a Storm Gathered (over Europe) but otherwise nothing good happened. The main themes are the Depression, the Poor, Abroad, and Other.

### CESSATION OF ROARING

As soon as the Thirties began people stopped Roaring, which proves that the Depression was serious. Indeed many people were so Depressed that they did not even bother to go to work. This caused Mass Unemployment – a Bad Thing.

Mayfly Keynes, the witty and scabrous economist (and partner in the Bloomsbury Group), thought of a helpful and rather Keynesian Alternative to Mass Unemployment, but as this contradicted the Treasury author* he wouldn't accept it.

---

* Doxy

*Mayfly Keynes*

The only Good Thing was that people in America were just as Depressed (if not more so) on account of their Inhibition about drinking alcohol. Some Bootleggers and Gangsters (such as 'Alco' Pone) were uninhibited, but criminal.

## Crisis Over Unemployment Benefit

During the Depression the Government had a Crisis, owing to a disagreement about whether there was any Benefit to Unemployment or not. When the Prime Minister Pansy Macdonald realised that he couldn't mend the rift in his cabinet caused by the row, he immediately set off for Buckingham Palace to make his tender resignation to the King.

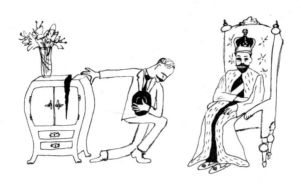

*Pansy Macdonald Resignating*

However King George refused to let Pansy resignate, telling him that the broken cabinet was nothing to worry about and could easily be replaced. Pansy therefore continued to be Prime Minister and returned to his Office.

## The Poor - A Central Theme

During the Thirties the Poor were continually disgruntled*, and hence prone to:

- Communism (The Opium of the People).
- Nasty incidents involving rickets.

Nevertheless, the Poor are a Central Theme of the Thirties.

---

*unemployed

## The Closure of the Pits

Merthyr Tydfil was a good example of a town in Wales, being next to some over-crowded Pits and full of poor people with terribly weak lungs. This is known as a Revolutionary Atmosphere and is a Bad Thing. In the end the Government completely lost its head and closed the Pits without warning. This action outraged many Socialists (who did not believe in suffocating Workers).

*Structurally Disgruntled Workers*

Many Welsh people in Merthyr Tydfil (and yllswhyrr in Wales) are structurally disgruntled to this day, sadly causing much of the country to be a hwtbyd of socialism, and thus (despite its memorable Pits) not a popular tourist destination.

## Orwell - A Radical Ineffectual

A large number of radical Ineffectuals in the Thirties argued that the Poor, although squalid, were very interesting subjects for books, pamphlets, photographs, paintings, poems, politics and perhaps even philosophy. A good example is Orwell, who was experienced in poverty himself, having been down (and out) in Paris (and London). He eventually found a job selling cockles (and mussels) on the Road to Wigan Pier.

Orwell's view was that the poor were squalid, but that if everyone became Socialists they might improve, though not until 1984 at the earliest. He also firmly believed that political power should on no account be transferred to animals (especially pigs), as can be seen from the title of his masterpiece *Animals Harm*.

## Abroad: Part of History

During the Thirties it emerged beyond all doubt that Abroad was part of History, as even places like Germany, Italy and Russia were sometimes Relevant (and thus came up in Exams). This was something* to do with Britain not being Top Nation any more.

---

* It is not known what

## WAVE OF FOOLISHNESS ACROSS EUROPE

Before continuing any further, it must first be stated how Sensible and Instinctively Sceptical the British People were. This can be seen in their **utter refusal** to embrace the fascist Oswald Mosley even though he was a quite superb orator and also remarkably dashing. Most other people of the period were very foolish, as is clearly demonstrated by the Wave of Foolishness (see below).

*British Scepticism*

## Foolish Germans

The Foolish Germans eagerly embraced the powerful rhetoric and neat moustache of Adolf Hitler, even though he was a known Fascist. This allowed Hitler to become their Great Dictator, and he immediately set about gathering a storm over Europe, by various means, fizz:

- He militarised Germany by handing out free Tanks, Jackboots and Waftluffes.
- He fanned the flames of resentment against France by claiming that it had pilfered millions of tonnes of Frankfurters.
- He impressed the Austrians so much with his Anschluss[*] that they finally admitted that Germany was Greater (which was what Hitler had been saying all along).

## Foolish Italians

The Italians were just as foolish as the Germans, and hence could not see through the charming but ill 'Duce', Dorito Mussolini, who led them straight into the Abyssinia.

---

[*] Bratwurst

*The Ill Duce*

Mussolini was a Fascist like Hitler, but he was somewhat less evil. This is demonstrated by his fondness for women and pasta, and the incompetence of his troops. On the other hand, his favourite subjects were Latin and Roman History.

## Foolish Russians

For some time after Linen's death Russia stayed backward, largely because Stalin foolishly kept putting off all his Plans for another Five Years. In the end, however, the Proletariat (Peasants) began to industrialise frantically on their own, producing miraculous quantities of pigs, iron and tanks in a very short time.

Nevertheless, they were unprepared for Hitler's invasion when it came and thus may aptly be termed foolish.

### APPEASEMENT: NOT SENSIBLE

Appeasement was the only not very sensible thing the British got involved in at this time. Neville Chambermaid, the unmanly British Prime Minister, was the top appeaser, and flew to Germany to appease Hitler *three times*. The third time, in Munich, Hitler pretended he was really appeased, and to prove it he scribbled a note on a white piece of paper and gave it to Chambermaid.

Chambermaid was so pleased that on his return he couldn't resist waving it around in an undignified manner, while stating the obvious (that he had in his hand a white piece of paper).

*Appeasement*

This behaviour was much frowned upon, especially by Churchill, the top frowner (or *dissident*) of the decade.

## START OF PRINCIPLE OF SELF-DETERMINATION

At one of their meetings Hitler suddenly turned to Chambermaid and shrieked, 'I myself am determined to occupy the Sudetenland!' This was known as the principle of self-determination, and was Hitler's favourite principle, used throughout the War (see invasions of Russia, Soviet Union, Holland, Netherlands, Low Countries etc).

## THE LIFE OF MADHATTA (MADHANDAS) GANDHI

Madhatta (Madhandas) Gandhi is one of the few really memorable Indians, and indeed had one of the most Memorable Figures of the Twentieth Century (along with Churchill). Gandhi's life should, however, be briefly summarised.

## YOUTH

As a young man, Gandhi lived in South Africa where he had generally been clothed in a suit, a tie and sometimes a hat, working by day as a lawyer and by night as an ambulance driver in the dangerous Boerwoer region. However, on the boat journey to India he changed into his Hallmark Loincloth and Trademark Bare Feet in order to appear more Indian and to show that he intended to be a Holy Man from then on.

*Hallmark Loincloth*

*Trademark Bare Feet*

### Indians: Responsible or Childish?

At that time there was a severe controversy raging in the Indian Subcontinent.* The Indians (known as Subjects) wanted Responsible Self-Government, but were offended by the British (known as Viceroys), who claimed that, as they were still somewhat prone to Mutinies and Black Holes, they were not Responsible but Childish.

---

* known by the British as the 'Raj' or the 'Jewel in the Crown', and by Indians either as 'India' or 'Pakistan', depending.

## Please be Civil (but Disobedient)

In response, Gandhi, whose Hallmark Loincloth and ability to walk on glowing coals in his Trademark Bare Feet had by now given him Moral Authority throughout the Raj, ordered all the Subjects to be Disobedient to the Viceroys, while always remaining Civil. (This was known as *Civil Disobedience*.)

Civil Disobedience was an excessively clever and annoying tactic, as the Viceroys were not allowed to fire their muskets into Gandhi or his Subjects* unless they were Uncivil, which they never were.

## Salt Lick

One good example of Gandhi's Civil Disobedience occurred when the Viceroys inhumanely banned the consumption of salt, which was the favourite foodstuff of most Indians.

In protest Gandhi marched hundreds of miles to a beach memorable for having salt instead of sand. On arrival he fell to his knees and politely (but firmly) licked the beach, even though he was in full view of a nearby Viceroy.

---

* Except at Official Massacres

*Gandhi's Salt Lick*

Gandhi was thus arrested and flung into prison. This is known as a Heavy-Handed Response, and is quite common in Imperial History.

### GANDHI RELEASED FROM PRISON

When Gandhi was released from prison, he was still very disobedient (though civil) and lost no time in chasing the Viceroys out of India. After their departure Civil Disobedience sadly deteriorated into Civil War, causing Pakistan and eventually Bangladesh (or East Pakistan).

### BEST FOREIGN ACTOR

Towards the end of his life, Gandhi was assassinated by an insane fanatic. He was posthumously awarded nine Oscars.

## The Spanish Civil War (by Orwell)

The famous author Orwell wrote this novel as a prelude to World War Too and to make a bit of extra money while he was down (and out) in Paris (and London). The story is memorable for inspiring thousands of Ineffectuals to sail over to Spain in order to fight against a General called Franco*, who was at that time trying to get promoted to Fascist Dictator. Sadly, many of the Ineffectuals were rather puny like Orwell himself, and so Frank easily overpowered them at Guernica.

*Picasso's Rankest Masterpiece*

Picasso painted an astonishingly modern and depressing painting depicting this scene, which is perhaps his rankest masterpiece.

---

* the Spanish version of Frank

## The Fornication Crisis

*The Fornication Crisis*

The Fornication Crisis occurred towards the end of the Thirties, when King Edward VIII betrayed his country and fornicated with Wallace Stevens, a glamorous American divorcée. The King was demoted to Duke and the ashamed couple emigrated to Paris (where such behaviour was *de rigueur*).

## The Bodyline Crisis

During the Depression the English cricket team made a Tour of Australia in an effort to cheer themselves up. For a while everything went well, with the English fast bowlers greatly amusing themselves and their team members by bowling the ball at 100mph straight at the heads of the main Australian batsman*, thus winning Famous Victories.

*Bodyline*

However, the Australians were not amused and thus ruined everything by accusing the English of being bad sports. The English replied that on the contrary it was the best sport they had ever had, far better than pheasant shooting or even pig-sticking. An Australian in the Pavilion was then overheard to remark, 'It's just not cricket!' This caused an Undiplomatic Incident and for a time it even seemed possible that Britain

---

* The Don Bradman

would disown Australia. In the end, however, it turned out that this wasn't possible at all, and things went back to normal.[*]

## Conclusion to The Thirties

As has been proven (see above), the Thirties were a Dreadful Decade from a historical point of view. However, they led straight to World War Too, which most Top Historians regard as an enormously violent occasion, and thus of more widespread appeal.

---

[*] Colonialism

## END OF CHAPTER TEST

**Answer a convincing majority of the following questions, in any language not of your choice.**

a) Are you willing to concede that the British have More Common Sense? If yes, please do so immediately (in the top left corner of your answer sheet).

b) Imagine for the briefest of moments that you are Neville Chambermaid. Are you ashamed of yourself?

c) Place in order of seniority: Hindu, Memsahib, Viceroy, Subject, Gandhi, Muslim. Which of these, in your opinion, is the hardest to spell? Why?

d) Come up with at least ten historical insights of breathtaking unoriginality. Do **not** write them down.

f) Choosing your words with careless abandon, describe either a Crisis or a Five Year Plan.

i) Write a email of indeterminate length to Adolf Hitler expressing nothing but your utter abhorrence.

# Chapter 3

# WORLD WAR TOO

TOP HISTORIANS REGARD World War Too as a Cataclysmic Event on an Immense Scale*, and therefore find it impossible to comprehend its Enormity even if they really concentrate.

*Top Historian - Unable to Comprehend*

---

* 9.6 on the Immense Scale

## Main differences between WWI and World War Too

- World War Too was *awesome*, as it had more tanks, Waftluffes, Panzies, atomic bombs, U-Boats, Das-Boots etc. The First World War, on the other hand, was *horrendous*, owing to the widespread popularity of trenches, trench foot, shell-shock, going over the top etc.

- World War Too was much less lyrical and thus poets tended to steer clear of it. (This may also be because puny types had all perished fighting against Franco – see above.)

- When World War Too was announced, not a single person threw their hat (or coat) in the air and rejoiced. This is called Cynicism. By contrast, many looked back on the outbreak of the First World War as the happiest moment of their lives. This is called Patriotism.

*Cynicism*

- World War Too contained the Holocaust which occurred due to Hitler's insane belief that Germany's problems were caused by Jews (since a suspiciously high proportion of them were *scapegoats*). As a punishment he sent them to kamps where they were all killed. Nobody can deny that this was the Holocaust, and was one of the Worst Things in the whole of history.

## CAUSES OF THE WAR

### 1 – GERMAN MILITARISM AND EXPANSIONISM

This is a deep-rooted and rather psychological cause. It explains the tendency of many Germans to militarise and expand when no one is looking in their direction. The Japanese are much the same.

### 2 – LEBENSRAUM

The German Volk (Hitler) fanatically believed that he deserved a more spacious Lebensraum. When he heard rumours about a castle in Eastern Europe with an enormous Lebensraum, he instantly invaded Poland.*

---

* Screaming 'I myself am determined to invade Poland.'

It is a curious aside that during the course of the War, the German Volk and his Gurbles (cronies) wasted much time drinking Sekt and hunting wild boars in luxurious Lebensraums. This was known as getting *schlossed*: a favourite Nasti Occupation occupation.

### 3 – POLAND

When Hitler offensively attacked Poland, the British Government immediately declared 'War!' This turned out to be an accurate prediction. The first few months, however, were dubbed the Phoney War as they mainly consisted of threatening phone calls and had very little actual fighting.

### 4 – THE GATHERING STORM

This cause includes all others and thus must be cited.

### NO QUISLING

A brief exception to the Phoney War was Hitler's conquest of Norway. On arrival, he quickly located a local Quisling (traitor) who wished to be his puppet. The Quisling was very unpopular in Britain, and signs appeared all over the country warning, 'No Quisling At Any Time'. This is an example of propaganda.

*Propaganda*          *Impropaganda*

### END OF PHONEY WAR

The Phoney War came to a sudden end when Hitler, in mid-phoney-conversation with Marshal Pétanque, suddenly decided to invade and occupy France and slammed down the receiver with overwhelming force.

### THE IMAGINOT (IMAGINARY) LINE...

In order to invade France, Hitler (in French: Itler) had to get past the exceptionally stupid Imaginot (Imaginary) Line which ran along the border with Germany.

*The Imaginot Line*

Although the French boasted that the Line was impénétrable, in reality it was not, for the following reasons:

a) It was Imaginary (Imaginot).

b) Even if it had not been Imaginot, the Germans would have been able to goose-step over it.

c) There was a huge gap in Belgium, which the French were hoping Itler wouldn't notice. However, Itler was a military genius, and thus noticed it right away. His tanks overran Belgium in just under ten minutes – a new German record.

## France is run over

Once they got past the Imaginot Line, it was easy for the Nastis to run over France, as the French did not yet have any Résistance. The BEFs (British soldiers) tried to stop their advance, but quickly came to the conclusion that the fight was unfair, due to the great speed, firepower and height of the enemy. They thus found themselves being heroically driven back towards Dunkirk (see below).

## Pétanque signs Armistice

When he had run over France, Itler forced Pétanque to sign an Armistice (Surrender) in a Eurostar train carriage (3ème Classe) in the Hall of Mirrors. This was humiliating for the French, but symbolic for the Germans.

According to the terms of the Armistice, the French were given a choice between submitting to a Vichy Régime (despicable but safe) and joining the Résistance (glorious but fatal). Most of the French population turned out to be despicable and safe rather than glorious and fatal, which is still very embarrassing for many French people even now. There were, however, a few notable exceptions such as Mata Hari and De Gaulle, who despite his name was often in England at the time.

Hitler also humiliated the French by forcing them to give up their traditional motto ('Lingerie, Fromagerie, Épicerie!') in favour of a humiliating new one ('Roquefort, Camembert, Brie!').

After this, Marshal Pétanque agreed to become a German and took charge of the Vichy Régime. He was wrongly very popular with the French at the time, but after the war De Gaulle (Of France) rightly commuted him to life imprisonment (for treason).

### DUNKIRK

Dunkirk is the opposite of D-Day and should not be interchangeable with Dunkerque except by professional historians. It occurred when some BEFs found themselves heroically stranded on a beach, and were therefore gloriously evacuated back home in dinghies, canoes, lilos and other craft.

*Dunkirk: the opposite of D-Day*

After Dunkirk, Churchill made a famous speech declaring that, 'In future, we will fight them on the beaches and in the hedges, in the corridors and on the landings etc etc.' This was judged to be his most stirring yet.

### The Waftluffes

When he had overrun France, Itler laughably decided to try to conquer Britain! He therefore sent over Messrs Schmidt und Schmidt (Germany's top two pilots) to have a Battle of Britain in their deadly Waftluffes (Spitfires).

*Messrs. Schmidt und Schmidt*

However, the Schmidts were gloriously defeated after the Finest Hour of fighting ever seen. *Never before had so many said 'Phew!' so much.*

When he lost the Battle of Britain Hitler tried to open peace negotiations with Churchill, offering him a large box of free Swas Stickers, as well as a Carte Blanche (to humiliate France whenever he felt the urge). Typically, however, Churchill shoved these items back in Hitler's evil-smelling teeth, where they belonged.

In response, Hitler proclaimed the Blitz.


### The Blitz

The Blitz was a terrifying ordeal full of WaftLuffes, Doodlebugs, Noodlebugs and even Stroodlebugs, but it is nevertheless memorable for being the most cheerful period in British History.

The Queen Mother was probably the most cheerful person of all, staunchly residing in Buckingham Palace, and smiling for the entire duration. She was henceforth much loved.

*The Queen Mother after a Noodlebug attack*

The Blitz caused Camaraderie and National Identity, but it was also responsible for fleas, Coventry Cathedral and overcrowded Tube Stations.

*Bomber Arthur Harris*

Bomber Arthur Harris was in charge of the equivalent of the Blitz in Germany, known as Strategic Bombing.

Bomber Arthur Harris was an English war hero (or villain, depending) who from an early age loved nothing more than to play with bombs. Hence he was christened Bomber by his parents.

*Bomber as an infant*

Until World War Too Bomber had never had a chance to play with any real bombs, but that all changed when Churchill appointed him National Bomber-in-Chief.

Bomber's main aim was to try to sap the morale of the German civilians. This was far too high, especially in a city called Dresden where civilians were unfairly enjoying themselves at operas and art galleries, and children were playing happily in the streets, *even though a World War was on*. Bomber argued that with just 20,000 bombs he could sap the morale of the Dresden civilians in one single night.

This turned out to be true, but Bomber is still a rather notorius figure (see Eunuch Powell for unilluminating comparison). Today it is generally concurred that civilians should not be bombed unless they a) live in Iraq or b) sign a form (available from the Post Office) promising not to sue.

### THE EASTERN FRONT

The Eastern Front occurred when Hitler stupidly learnt from History (e.g. Napoleon) and thus invaded Russia. As is well known, Russia can only be conquered by means of Mongolian Ponies*, due to its Frozen Wastes and Scorched Earth Policy. Hitler named his invasion Barbarossa after a girl he had fancied in his Hitler Youth.

When Hitler invaded, Stalin was so surprised that he hid under the Kremlin and drank nothing but Molotov Cocktails for three days, thus allowing the Nastis to swiftly overrun the west of the country. However, during this time he became Supreme Commander, to everybody's relief (especially the Russians').

---

* c.f. Genghis Khan and the Tartars' Horse

*Nothing but Molotov Cocktails*

As Supreme Commander (and Dictator) Stalin dictated two main policies:

a) Any Soviet (or Russian) soldier caught yielding more than a verst* would be shot immediately.

b) The Russian (or Soviet) Winter would eventually defeat the invaders. (This had been a traditional policy in Russia since Napoleon and his army froze stiff in

---

* Inch

Moscow in the middle of a performance of the 1812 symphony.)

Stalin's policies were especially effective at the Battle of Stalingrad, where an entire German Korpse was annihilated. This was the turning point of the War, as after it all other German Korpses turned round and began to march home.


## New Theatre: Afrika

In the meantime a new theatre (of combat) opened in Afrika, due to the presence of the German Rommel with his Afrika Korpse, and Monty Don, the popular British hero. The Afrikan Theatre was the only chivalrous part of the War, owing to the fact that Rommel was a gentleman and not really a real Nasti and also had a rather high regard for Monty Don (and vice-versa).

The war in Afrika is also memorable for the importance of tactics and strategy. Rommel was very good at tactics (battles), but Monty Don was better at strategy (wars) and thus won in the end. Monty Don's victory in Afrika was an excessively Good Strategy, as it meant that the underbelly of Europe (Italy) could now be invaded.

## Pearl Harbour: A Stroke of Good Fortune

Pearl Harbour was a Stroke of Good Fortune for Britain, but a Day of Infamy for America. It occurred when some Japanese Kamikazes* attacked the US Fleet, forcing America to enter the War (on the British team). This made Ultimate Victory certain, owing to America's Industrial Might and limitless supply of G.I. Joes.

*A stroke of good fortune*

Before Pearl Harbour, Americans had been pretending that the War was none of their business, and were thus prospering unfairly.

---

*lunatics

After the Stroke of Good Fortune, there was a War in the Pacific against Japan, involving a wave of unmemorable American Naval Victories (mainly on the Pacific Atoll*). This was about Midway through the conflict.

## D-Day

D-Day was the exact opposite of Dunkirk (see above) and thus consisted of a glorious invasion of some Norman beachheads in Omaha, France, using an assortment of craft.

*The opposite of Dunkirk*

After D-Day, Ultimate Victory became even more certain than it was before, as there were then only a few hedgerows lying between Allied Forces and Berlin, where Hitler was already hiding insanely in his Bünker.

---

* Ocean

## The Final Phase

The Final Phase of the War in Europe occurred after D-Day and as is traditional consisted of a headlong retreat (by the Germans), and a headlong advance (by the Allies).

The only exception was the Battle of the Bulge, when some Americans were unexpectedly counter-attacked in the Ardennes Pâté region, briefly causing them to retreat (though not headlong).

## Allied Victory

Even though they had been severely delayed en route by the need to carry out Rape and Pillage Operations the Russians (or Soviets) were the first to arrive in Berlin. This was widely considered a Bad Thing, as it caused increased Russian influence, and hence the Cold War, poison umbrellas, Russian salad etc

When he realised that defeat was certain, Hitler became even more insane than usual, marrying his long term partner Eva Brawn and then suddenly shooting himself after the ceremony. In Germany this is known as a shotgun wedding. It prompted a nasty Wave of Suicides throughout the Bünker, after which the only officer still alive (Donutz) surrendered unconditionally.

*A shotgun wedding*

## VE DAYS IN EUROPE AND JAPAN

It was then officially time for VE Day in Europe. VE Day in Japan soon followed, after two American bombs controversially vaporised the island.

## THE END OF WORLD WAR TOO

It was thus the end of World War Too.*

---

*And the start of the Post War, the Cold War etc etc

## End of Chapter Test

**Provide war-like responses to any five questions. (HINT: You need not confine yourself to those listed below.)**

a) 'Arbeit Macht Frei!' Discuss.

b) Write a postcard to your mother from Stalingrad, omitting no detail of your hellish experiences.

c) Did we fight them on the beaches, behind the bike sheds, both, or neither? With hindsight, was Churchill's prediction justified?

d) Describe the emotions of a torpedoed cruiser (as it sinks slowly to eternal rest on the ocean floor).

e) 'Balding, fat, and frequently smoking a cigar.' How accurate do you find this assessment of Winston Churchill?

f) Using only unavailable evidence, determine whether D-Day or Dunkirk was more heroic.

g) Account (with scorn) for the terrific ease with which Hitler overran France and Belgium.

## Chapter 4

# THE POST WAR

———⚬⚬⚬———

THE POST WAR began as soon as VE Day in Japan was signed. It is comprehensively illustrated below.

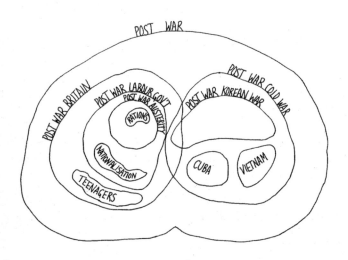

*The Post War Explained*

## The Cold War

As can be seen (underleaf) the Cold War was one of the most important subsets of the Post War. It was against Russia (or America, depending), and consisted mainly of International Tension and Gorilla* Wars in distant lands† around the globe. Gorilla Wars were always fought by Proxees‡.

The Cold War is so called because of Russia's Continental Climate, with its alternating pattern of very cold winters and very damp autumns.

### Causes

The so-called Cold War was started by Russian (or Soviet) aggression. The main example of this was the Soviet (or Russian) Occupation of many quite significant countries in Eastern Europe, such as Poland, Hungary and several besides. The Russian (or Soviet) Leader Stalin then insensitively merged the countries into a single Bloc, to their great Shoc and Horror.

When he saw what Stalin had done, Chruchill commented that

---

* Uncivilised

† such as Asia and Africa

‡ Asians and Africans

an Iron Curtain had descended on the continent.[*] This was a false but memorable quotation, and thus a good example of a metaphor.

## Teams

The American[†] team name in the Cold War was NATO, which means 'I win' in Latin. The Russians called their team 'Warsaw Pact'. This was less catchy, and could not even be made into an Acronym, as it was found that 'WP' was pronounced differently by the Poles and the Hungarians (who thus became mutually incomprehensible).

*Mutually Incomprehensible*

---

[*] Europe
[†] and British

The Korean War is a subset of the Cold War and thus also the Post War. It is firmly believed by Koreans to have been a Significant Conflict, yet it is hardly memorable at all. This is called a Paradox, and even top Historians are still frequently baffled by it.

*Brilliant Equations*

The Korean War was caused when after World War Too nobody apart from Japan wanted to have Korea, which in those days was merely an undersized peninsular on the other side of the world.

Unfortunately, Korea could not be given to the Japanese as they were in disgrace owing to their kamikaze* behaviour during the War.

It was therefore agreed that Russia and America should divide Korea amongst themselves, with each Superpower responsible for precisely half of the peninsular, *no more and no less*. However, the top mathematicians on both sides could not agree about the best way to divide a peninsular in half, especially one with such an awkward shape.

Finally the American General MacArthur demonstrated by means of some brilliant equations that a parallel line must be used. After drawing 37 parallel lines in the intense heat and over some rough terrain, MacArthur finally drew one in the right place. This was named the 38th parallel.

The Russian half was in the Communist North, while the Americans took the South of the country, essentially a more Capitalist area.

Up to this point no one had become tense enough to escalate an actual war. However, this changed due to the thoughtless action of some Russians, who suddenly encroached the Americans

---

* crazy

in the South while they were looking the other way. This was clearly Tantamount to Encroachment, and made a War inevitable (by International Law).

*Gloriously All But Wiped Out*

In the end the Korean War turned out to be quite unfair, due to millions of Chinese intruders suddenly joining on the Russian team. It was therefore not very glorious, except for the brave conduct of some Double Gloucesters from Britain, who were gloriously all but wiped out on a hillside.

### AFTERMATH

Owing to the British and the Americans not winning the Korean War, North Korea was able to develop Axes of Evil – A Bad Thing. The South, however, concentrated on making cheap televisions, microwaves and fridges, and thus rightly prospered.

## DEATH OF STALIN

In the middle of the Post War Stalin died, as he had Purged all the doctors in Russia and there were none left to write out his prescriptions. Even though he is dead, Stalin is extremely significant for the following reasons:

a) He was almost certainly the Top Dictator of all time, responsible for at least three times as many dictations* as his closest rival Hitler.

*Stalin, Top Dictator*

---

* around 30,000,000

b) Although overall he was a Very Bad Thing, he became a Good Thing during World War Too against the Nastis.

c) His legacy* lives on (c.f. Saddam).

### Post War Labour Government

After World War Too Churchill was very tired and decided to take a short break from being Prime Minister. His successor was a well-known Labour voter called Clementine Attlee.

A majority of ordinary British people were secretly quite pleased to have a Labour Prime Minister for a change as they wanted to win the peace as well as the war, which was one of the Labour Party's top policies.

### Wave of Bevs

Attlee's first policy was a Wave of Bevs. The first Bev was Beverage, a Headmaster who wrote a Report on Five Giants† who were then roaming about the country. Beverage wrote in his Report that all Five could do much better, and that Want especially

---

* moustache
† The Giants were named Want, Ignorance, Disease, Squalor and Idleness.

should pull his socks up as the others all followed his example. When two other Bevs[*] of the period, read the Report they were immediately galvanised to create BHS[†], an institution which slew the Giants by giving them a giant overdose of Free Operations and Painkillers. From that moment on everyone in the country lived in a State of Welfare.

BHS was a Major Reform of the Twentieth Century, and thus could well be considered the main achievement of the Bevs.

### Post War Austerity

Austerity consisted mainly of Rations, which were tiny amounts of bacon, eggs, and lard and were all anyone was allowed to eat at the time.

*Coupons*

---

*Aneurism and Neigh
† Bevs' Health Service

Fat people were not even allowed to eat rations and were given coupons instead.

Rations were an unpopular policy, as most people enjoyed normal food and did not find lard at all to their taste, even in small quantities.

## NATIONALISATION: A MAJOR IF UNEVENTFUL REFORM

Nationalisation was a Major if Uneventful Reform of the British Industries.* Attlee was a Socialist, and thus took the view that Coal, Steel and Baked Beans were Goods, and should be shared equally among all Socialists rather than belonging only to Capitalists. The Capitalists disagreed On Principle but In Practice there was nothing they could do.

Although Nationalisation was certainly a Major Reform and always comes up in Exams about the Post War, very little actually changed as the average person remained inefficient, short of coal and prone to power cuts.

---

* Coal, Steel and Baked Beans

## EEK (European Ekonomic Kommunity)

Soon after the War the General Of France* declared that Europe should change its name to EEK, and also that all Nations should be abolished and become Member States instead. De Gaulle's view was that every Nation wanted to become Top Nation†, whereas Member States could harmoniously indulge in their Common Interests, such as the Common Agricultural Police and solving Acronyms.

However, it turned out that nobody found the Common Agricultural Policy nearly as interesting as wars or even rivalries, and thus EEK sadly deteriorated into the *Utterly Unmemorable European Union* (UUEU).

---

### The Utterly Unmemorable European Union (UUEU) Fig 2.2.1 (a)

*Everything to do with the European Union (EU) is Utterly Unmemorable (UU), except for the fact that one should always write about it in Italics, in a separate Box, and include a Fig.*

---

\* De Gaulle

† thus causing wars, rivalries, embargos, lumbagos etc

## THE FESTIVAL OF BRITAIN

The Festival of Britain was held in a brilliant new architectural eyesore on the South Bank of London, in protest against Austerity. A good time was had by all and free toffee apples were distributed to the entire nation, including the fat. This caused a large amount of Jubilation, but also fuelled Excessive Optimism about the Economic Future of the country (which was ironically rather bleak owing to Britain not owning most of the world any more).

*Excessive Jubilation*

## CHURCHILL RETURNS

The Festival put a stop to Austerity once and for all, and to prove it Churchill returned to power. Although he was well over seventy and thus prone to strokes[*], he retained his sense of fun.[†] This is proved by the fact that he promptly invented the game British Bulldogs, at which he was World Champion five years in a row.

*British Bulldog Champion*

Churchill rather disapproved of rations, preferring to indulge his appetites rather than practise self-restraint. He urged the people of Britain to follow his example and enjoy life by:

- Smoking very good cigars
- Sampling the pleasures of Monte Carlo
- Only having very minor strokes

---

[*] like Linen
[†] unlike Linen

## More of a Global Figure

By this time Churchill had more of a Global than a Domestic figure, and thus spent most of the time when he was meant to be in his Office abroad. Although he left a sign on the door saying, 'Back in 10 minutes', no one really believed him.

Churchill's appointed heir at that time was Anthony Eden, but he usually ended up being disappointed (when Churchill unexpectedly returned to his office, or turned out only to have had a minor stroke).

In the end, however, Churchill unwisely suffered a Major Stroke which according to the Rules meant he had to resign.

## A Weak New Prime Minister

The new Prime Minister Anthony Eden was weak and thus developed an embarrassing Sinai condition as soon as he stepped into his Office.

## The Swizz Crisis

Eden's Sinai problems severely affected his judgement, especially when the wold's top canal* became blocked with Egyptian

---

* The Swizz Canal

Nationalists who had dived into it in order to secure it for their Nation*. They were encouraged in this by King Nassa, who was a Dam Nuisance and on no account an Acronym, and for these two very good reasons should neither be Capitalised nor confused with NASA.

This caused Eden to have a full-blown Swizz Crisis, during which he ordered several thousand British troops to go on a rash Expedition (to unblock the canal).

*Egyptian Nationalists*

---

* Egypt

However, Eden had forgotten that Britain was no longer Top Nation and thus not allowed to behave in an unacceptable manner. He was therefore permanently humiliated* when the UNited states ordered him to cease firing on the Egyptians in the canal and return home immediately.

## 'Never Had It So Good'

The Swizz Crisis made British People insecure about whether they were still Great or not, and to make matters worse a *Run on Sterling* occurred at the same time. The exact meaning of this phrase is not clear (except to obscure historians and economists), but there can be no doubt that it was a Bad Thing, and quite Humiliating.

The new Prime Minister Macmillan therefore decided to make a brilliant speech, informing everybody who would listen that they *had never had it so good.* He then proved beyond reasonable doubt that it was not so very long ago[†] that nobody had possessed hoovers, toasters or even nylon. This was very true and brilliant because it made the British people feel much better about everything – A Good Thing for the Government.

---

* and forced to step down from his Office
† i.e. in the Trenches or Victorian Slums

## Post War Boom Eventually Causing Teenagers...

As is quite demonstrable by means of statistics, there was a Boom in the production of Babies after the War, stimulated by the return home of the soldiers. Babies were popular with families at the time because unlike bacon and lard they were not rationed and so legal even in large helpings.

However, parents were far too busy rebuilding Britain and stimulating each other after the war to realise that their babies would become Teenagers. Teenagers were first seen in the Post War and thus were a new phenomenon (as historically there had only been Masters, Misses or Child Labourers).

*Teenagers*

A very important fact to remember about the Post War Babies is that they were the first generation ever with no first-hand experience of war, bereavement or even hardship, and therefore were prone to Low Moral Standards.

### THE TELEVISED CORONATION CHICKEN

The Coronation Chicken was an enormous fowl transported from the Indian sub-continent in order to feed the guests at the televised coronation of Queen Elizabeth.

*The Coronation Chicken Arriving at Portsmouth*

As the coronation was to be broadcast to all her Subjects around the world, the Queen chose to dress in fine traditional style, in a purple and ermine frock (which she was very careful not to stain with the sauce). Her husband Philip, who was somewhat German and therefore not allowed to be King, was very much part of the background.

## CULTURAL IMPERIALISM...

In the Post War a new kind of Imperialism started, which is still happening now. This is called Cultural Imperialism and is a Bad Thing as all the Cultural Imperialists, such as Ronald McDonald's and Elvis Presley, are American (and thus Obese), whereas in the past they were British (and thus not Obese). The aim of American Cultural Imperialists is to export American Values* to the rest of the world.

*American Values*

---

* Obesity and Sexuality

McDonald's's main export was Obesity. As a young man Elvis exported mainly Sexuality, but this changed towards the end of his life.

## Surfeit of Cheeseburgers

Elvis tragically died of a surfeit of Macdonald's's cheeseburgers. This is particularly ironic as one of his earliest hits was called *Hot Dog*.

Elvis' death is unusual for a legendary figure, most of whom are killed by insane fanatics (c.f. Gandhi, John Linen and JFK Kennedy). For this reason there are many insane fanatics who find it impossible to believe that Elvis *is* dead, arguing that, on the contrary, he *lives on*.

## Conclusion to Post War

Overall, the Post War was quite a nostalgic period of history, and hence remains popular today, even though compared to many other wars there was very little actual fighting.

## END OF CHAPTER TEST

**Approach the following questions in a spirit of Post War Crisis. Ration your answers accordingly.**

a) Confuse and contrast at least one (or two) of the following: NATO and EEK, Burgess and Maclean, Koreans and Japanese. If none of the above appeals, try Bevan, Bevin, Baffin, Bivin and Bovril.

b) Illustrate the post-war decline in moral standards (by cheating, lying, spitting, littering etc).

c) Focus intently on the Swizz Crisis, giving seven reasons for your action.

d) Write a short cultural history of the cheeseburger. Entitle the piece simply: 'A short cultural history of the cheeseburger'.

f) Why is it so difficult to discourse entertainingly on the subject of Clement Attlee?

g) Decline to conjugate NATO.

h) Comment (but not too loudly) on the Korean War.

# Chapter 5

# THE SIXTIES

### INTRODUCTION

The history of the Sixties must first be divided simplistically into two parts: Social History and Anti-Social History.

Social History is much easier and includes the Beatles, Sex and Polka Dot Bikinis. Anti-Social History is more traditional and is mostly about War, Politics and Atrocities. The Berlin Wall, Pol Pot and Vietnam (not in that order) are good examples of Anti-Social History.

*An example of social history*

Another very sophisticated (yet intelligent) point to make about the Sixties is that they did not begin all of a sudden, but emerged gradually from the Fifties where they had their roots.

## FREEDOM

In the Sixties most people started Wearing Jeans, Swinging and Behaving Sexually in public spaces. Doing all of these things at the same time is known as Freedom, and is excessively liberating.

*Freedom: Excessively Liberating*

## The Beatles

The Beatles were a rock* band in the Sixties, and consisted of the four most popular men in the world. Indeed they were even more popular than Jesus, especially among teenage girls.

The Beatles taught the British public, even previously quite stiff people, how to rock†. John Linen (no relation of Linen) was the top rock‡ in the band, on account of being the only one who could rock, n' roll, and sing at the same time, even while having a lie-in in America with his wife Yoyo Coco.

When John Linen finally n'rolled out of bed and left his apartment, he was predictably assassinated by an insane fanatic, but Yoyo and his Memory live on. It is probable that the latter will live on forever.

## Anti-Sexual History

Some people in the Sixties did not wear jeans or behave sexually in public spaces even though they were allowed to. The two top examples are the poet Philip Gherkin, who was too busy

---

* n' roll

† n' roll

‡ n' roller

swearing at his Mum and Dad to notice what was going on*, and the prune Mary Whitehouse, who was more interested in keeping her T.V. clean.

*Mary Whitehouse*

## The Lady Chatterley Ban

Lady Chatterley was a Notorious Peeress who was completely banned until she was released on bail after a famous trial in the Sixties. She immediately went to visit her red-blooded gamekeeper Mellors in order to have some graphic scenes with him. This was inappropriate as Mellors was low-born and also her husband Lord Chatterley was confined to a wheelchair so could not join in.

---

* especially after 1963

## The Perfumo Affair

John Perfumo was probably the opposite of Phillip Gherkin. He was the Colognial Secretary, and unusually sexual even for the Sixties. When it was found that he had been having a Perfumo Affair with the KGB agent Helen Keller, he was forced to resign. This left a lasting whiff of scandal in the Corridors of Power.

## Homosexual Practice Legalised

In the Sixties it became legal for Homosexuals to practise. This was a Good Thing, as it led to an immediate improvement in British standards of Homosexuality which had fallen well behind those of other nations such as The Nether Regions, Holland, The Low Countries etc.

## Hippies

Hippies were common in the Sixties, owing to a widespread combination of Hippie Culture and Facial Hair. Hippies believed that flowers possessed great power and should be dropped on enemies instead of Atomic Bombs. However they were unable to prove this and thus gradually lost their influence.[*]

---

[*] but not their facial hair

As it was some time* after his first brilliant speech, Macmillan flew to Africa at the start of the Sixties in order to make another one. In it he sang to the Africans that the 'winds they were a-changing' on their continent.

*The Winds A-Changing*

At first the Africans were puzzled, as Macmillan had only been in the country for a few minutes and it was an exceptionally still day. However, the educated ones soon realised Macmillan had been talking in semaphores, and that what he really meant was that they would be completely on their own† from then on.

---

* several years, to be precise
† Independent

## WAVE OF INDEPENDENCE DAYS

After this there was a Wave of Independence Days, causing the British Empire to shrink into a Commonwealth.

When this happened everyone was ashamed, though there was a dispute about what they should be ashamed about. Some people were ashamed about their Imperial Past, while others argued that their Imperial Past had been highly glorious and were ashamed of their Commonwealth Future instead.

However, both parties agreed that moustaches were no longer seemly in a Post-Imperial World, except under extreme circumstances.*

*Moustaches: not seemly except under extreme circumstances*

---

* such as the Middle East

The Vietnam War was a particularly excessive example of Anti-Social History. However, Vietnam was a perfect place to have a Cold War as:

a) Like Korea it had an Communist North and a Capitalist South.

b) It contained large numbers of Proxees.[*]

In the end, though, the Vietnam War turned out not to be at all glorious, despite the use of some highly questionable tactics.

The most questionable tactic of all was Agent Orange, who sprayed all the trees in the country with a poison that burned off all their leaves, his plan being to expose all the enemy Proxees hiding underneath. At first the plan was highly successful, as after the spraying most of the enemy Proxees were not only exposed, but also dead (even down to the smallest women and tiniest children among them).

However, there turned out to be more Proxees than anyone had thought possible. The Americans were thus outnumbered and

---

[*] Vietnamese

forced to surrender humiliatingly to the Proxee Commander, a local beauty named Miss Saigon.*

*Agent Orange - A Questionable Tactic*

### AUSTIN POWERS

Austin Powers was nothing to do with Vietnam. On the contrary, he was a top American spy who was shot down over Siberia by Premier Khrushchev, the Uncouth Soviet Leader. Powers claimed that he had merely been doing a Reconnaissance on the weather to find out if it was really as cold and snowy as the Russians (or Soviets) claimed. However, Premier Khrushchev did not believe a word of this, and had Powers imprisoned with a local Ghoul-Hag.

---

* strictly speaking, this occurred in the next chapter (*The Seventies*)

## Uncouth Episode

This caused a lot of Global Tension, made even worse when Premier Khrushchev tactlessly used his shoe to swat a fly which had settled on the Soviet Delegation in New York during a speech by JFK Kennedy.

From then on many observers (including even Russians) felt that Khrushchev was far too Uncouth for the International Stage and should henceforth confine his activities to the provincial pantomime circuit in Siberia.

## Bay of Pigs – A Debacle

In revenge for Khrushchev's insult, JFK Kennedy sent a team of CIA agents disguised as pigs on a débacle to Cuba to Castrate Fido, who was a close friend of Khrushchev's from his cigar smoking youth. However, the débacle ended in failure, as without air support the pigs did not know where to go and ended up falling into a deep bay where they drowned.

Khrushchev and his allies pretended to be very cross about this, but really they thought it was hilarious (and made a lot of jokes about Swinish Capitalists). JFK Kennedy, on the other hand, was genuinely furious, though the only revenge he could think of for the time being was to impose a crippling Lumbago on Cuba.

*The Bay of Pigs Débacle*

## TOP CRISIS

Soon after this the Top Crisis in the history of the planet occurred, and for a few fateful hours caused most of the world to hold their breath (while being glued to their radios).

The Crisis began when JFK Kennedy began to suspect that Premier Khrushchev was installing Nuclear Missiles on his doorstep, which for some reason was in Cuba. He therefore organised an immediate face-off with Premier Khrushchev, during which (according to a passing Ambassador) the two men's eyeballs actually touched.

*Face-off*

Without blinking once, JFK Kennedy told Khrushchev that if the Soviet Missiles came anywhere near his doortep he would start World War III in no uncertain terms. Khrushchev agreed to take them back home with him, but managed to save part of his face (which had been severely damaged by this encounter) by persuading JFK Kennedy to remove his own less memorable missiles from Russia's doorstep, for some reason then in Turkey.

From this time on until his death JFK Kennedy was rarely seen without a young, good-looking and charismatic smile on his face, while Khrushchev grew steadily older and yet more ignominious.

## Assassination of JFK Kennedy, causing an Airport and a Memorable Day, but not a Date

Some time later the young JFK Kennedy was seated tragically in a cavalcade riding through the city of Dallas, when two shots unexpectedly rang out, causing the President to collapse charismatically into the lap of his glamorous wife, who immediately announced to the world that he was dead.

Outside America, this event is mainly memorable for the fact that everyone in America can remember exactly what they were doing when they heard the first shot (even if it was something altogether pedestrian like tooth-brushing, peeling an onion or just walking). However many cannot remember the exact date, which for some reason turned out not to be memorable.

*At the time of the first shot*

## Post-Humus Phase of JFK Kennedy's life

Once his assassin Lee Harvey Oswald (surname unknown) had been thoroughly executed, JFK Kennedy's life entered a Post-Humus Phase. This involved the following Post-Humus Honours:

a) The construction of the top Airport in the country, named JFK Kennedy Airport.

b) The construction of the top Cape in the country, named Cape Kennedy.

### Concise (yet Pungent) Summary

In the end, many Americans felt that the assassination of such a young, good-looking and charismatic President was an unbelievably tragic event. Others did believe it, but agreed that it was tragic.

### EEK

Around this time the British Prime Minister visited the French Leader De Gaulle* to ask him if Britain could join EEK, but in mid-conversation De Gaulle suddenly turned on him and yelled

---

* Of France

'VETO!' (which means 'I despise you!' in Latin). This was very wrong of De Gaulle, but unfortunately it was also his Right, so there was nothing to be done.

## THE SPACE RACE

The Space Race was the least traditional part of the Cold War, and consisted of two astronauts: a Russian Bear called Yogi Gagarin and an American equivalent called Neil Armstrong.

The aim of the Space Race was to orbit the planet* and/or thrust a National Flag dramatically into the moon.

At first Yogi seemed to be winning, as he completed a full orbit of the planet† before Neil had even pulled on his moon boots. However, Neil was able to overtake him on the way to the moon as he had become somewhat corrupted by success and was thus not as fast as he used to be.

After thrusting his National‡ Flag dramatically into the moon, Neil commented memorably that 'Getting to the Moon is just a tiny step for Mankind, but it would be a giant leap for a single Man.' This is oft-quoted but true.

---

* Earth

† Earth

‡ American

*A Giant Leap for a Single Man*

## 1966 and all that...

At the start of 1966 morale in Britain was low, since everybody was thinking about the Humiliating Conquest which they had suffered 900 years before at the hands of the Normans.* Historians were particularly afflicted, as there had not been a single Truly Memorable Date since that time.

The situation was not improved by the behaviour of the Germans, who had callously forgotten how Churchill had humiliated them on the Beaches and were prospering unfairly.

---

* another word for Germans

Luckily, however, the German football team came over for a World Cup Final on some Hallowed Turf near the Twin Towers of Wembley Cathedral. This turned out to be an incredibly memorable event, since the Germans lost owing to a heroic but controversial trick performed by one of the English players with his hat.

*Germans prospering unfairly*

This caused someone to memorably commentate that they thought it was all over, *and then it was*. The Queen was thrilled and thus spontaneously promoted the English captain Sir Bobby More to Archbishop of Canterbury (as a reward for his faithful service on and off the pitch).

In retrospect it is not surprising that the English team were victorious, as every man among them was a Hero, while the Germans had none at all on their side. However, they suffered defeat graciously, and agreed to return the oldest football in the world, which a thief had stolen at the Battle of Hastings.

*Bolus Homo Venit**

Hence it is said that on this day 'The Football Came Home.'

## CONCLUSION

Four years later, and not a moment too soon, the Sixties came to an abrupt end.

---

\* The Football Came Home

## End of Chapter Test

**Answer as many or as few questions as you can. Feel free to scratch, stroke or even lick the person sitting in front of you.**

a) What (if anything) is so funny about the Bay of Pigs?

b) Place in approximate order of sexuality: John Perfumo, Philip Gherkin, John Linen, The Nether Regions, Lady Chatterley.

c) 'J.F.K. Kennedy was the thirty-fifth President of the United States, serving from 1961 until his assassination in 1963.' Discuss.

d) In your view, how should the European Union go about making itself more memorable? Answers in acronyms only.

e) Write an eye-witness account of Lady Chatterley, leaving nothing to the imagination.

f) Was 1966 a vain attempt to over-compensate (for Loss of Empire, teenagers, General De Gaulle etc).

g) Analyse the widespread appeal of Proxee Wars.

## Chapter 6

# THE SEVENTIES – A BAD THING

### INTRODUCTION

THE SEVENTIES WERE a Bad Thing, with a Surfeit of Sheiks, Economics and Acronyms*, sometimes even all four at the same time (though not necessarily in that order). However, one Good Thing was the discovery of large reserves of Natural Gas in the North Sea, which proved (beyond reasonable doubt) that Britain was still Great.

*Natural Gas*

---

* S.E.A. (though not necessarily in that order)

It must also be noted that the Seventies were by far the least memorable decade in modern history so far, and thus this chapter should be quite short.

## The Fuel Crisis: A Bad Thing

The Fuel Crisis was a stereotypical event of the period, as it contained a lot of Economics as well as one of the top Acronyms in the world* and several Sheikhs.

It occurred when the Sheikhs suddenly hid all their fuel under some camels and refused to hand it over to the West. This was typically Crude behaviour, and caused a major fuel shock around the world.

*Typically Crude Behaviour*

---

* O.P.E.C. (Oil & Petrol Equals Cash)

One result of the Fuel Crisis was Stagflation – an Economic Condition and thus a dreadful waste of everybody's time and money. Luckily, however, the condition passed by before it ruined everything for good.

## DECIMATION

Decimation was a highly controversial economic policy of the Seventies. Most ordinary British people were quite opposed to being decimated, but it happened anyway because they were not trained Economists nor even politicians and thus did not know what was best.

According to trained economists and politicians Decimation was A Good Thing because:

a) It would make O-level Maths* much easier.

b) It would reduce queues in shops.

c) Most people in the rest of Europe had already been decimated†, in some cases hundreds of years ago, and it had never done them any harm.

---

* on no account to be confused with GCSE Maths
† i.e. during the French Revolution, the Thirty Years' War etc

*Decimation*

However, an unforeseen consequence of Decimation in Britain was that many old people could never get used to it and thus moaned about it for the rest of their lives – A Very Tiresome Thing.

### WINTER OF DISCONTENT: A SUCCESSFUL POLICY

The most successful economic policy of the Seventies was the Winter of Discontent, which was masterminded by Prime Minister James Callaghan. During the winter in question, polls showed that 99.6% of British people were very discontented, which was even better than Callaghan himself had hoped for. However, Callaghan did not foresee that the Dead would Remain Unburied during the Winter, which was quite a medieval situation and thus Unpopular.

For this reason Callaghan lost the General Election shortly afterwards to Margaret Thatcher, an Iron Lady*.

### IRELAND: ANOTHER BAD THING

The main cause of the surfeit of bombs in Britain in the Seventies was the Irish Question, which had still not been correctly answered.

*The Irish Question*

However, by this time it was even more difficult to answer the Question than it had been before as everyone had forgotten

---

* See following chapter

what it was. Some people thought it was 'What is the opposite of Ulster?' but others felt it was almost certainly 'Do I really need to learn Gaelic?' A small minority of Anarchists claimed the true Irish Question was 'What is the Irish Question?' but nobody paid any attention.

Apart from violence, the main tactic of both the Irish and the British was Acronyms. The most memorable Irish acronym is I.R.A. (Irish Revolutionary Acronym) and the most memorable British one is R.A.C. (Royal Acronymous Constabulary). However, most historians agree that the Irish one is more memorable. It should also be noted that Eire (pronounced I.R.A.) is the Irish word for I.R.A. (pronounced Eire).

The highlight of the Seventies in Ireland was probably Bloody Sunday, which occurred when some British Soldiers shot dead some unarmed Irish Civilians and then hotly denied it. This gave everybody in both countries a lot to talk about and caused a Wave of Enquiries which continues to this day

### Eunuch Powell

Eunuch Powell was a rabid British politician of the Seventies who, after declaring that he was none other than Notorius, irresponsibly dressed up as a Roman Emperor and made a speech in which he claimed that many rivers (including the Tiber and even perhaps the Ouse) were foaming with blood. This caused Mass Hysteria as well as Racism, and as is the case with many metaphors was not even remotely true.

*Eunuch Powell*

In response the militaristic feminist German Greer wrote *The Male Enoch*, in which she famously argued that all men were basically Enochs.

## Pol Pot and Idi Amin

Pol Pot (Asian) and Idi Amin (African) were dictators who despite their silly names were able to rise to the top and kill huge numbers of people. Pol killed mainly Asians and so did Idi. Pol sometimes wore Rouge, especially in front of a Khamera.

## Ayatollah* Khomeini

The memorable Ayatollah Khomeini became Leader of Iran after leading an Iranian Revolution against King Shah, who was haughty and did not love his people (and thus a Tyrant).

*Throwing away the key*

Sadly, it soon turned out that the Ayatollah was also haughty and did not love his people. Even worse, he was fundamentally a Muslim and thus A Very Very Very Bad Thing. However it was too late to oust him as as he had locked all his people (whom he did not love) in a Mosque and thrown away the key.

---

* Monster

# Conclusion

See Introduction (above).

## END OF CHAPTER TEST

**Give economical yet tedious answers to any or all of the following questions.**

a) Recreate Bloody Sunday, using only the plasticine provided. Do **not** allow the colours to become mixed up.

b) Were Pol Pot and Idi Amin mere coincidences or the result of specific historical circumstances?

c) Why does O.P.E.C.*?

d) 'Decimation, Decimation, Decimation.' Did any politicians say this in the Seventies? Why not?

e) Reflect privately on either the Iranian Revolution or the discovery of Natural Gas in the North Sea. Which do you prefer?

g) How serious is a surfeit of economics?

---

* Oil & Petrol Equal Cash

Chapter 7

# THE EIGHTIES

## INTRODUCTION

THE EIGHTIES TOOK place against a background of crumbling ideals, showy affluence and Duran Duran. In the foreground were Margaret Thatcher, Ronald Reagan* and Gorby.

## THE IRON LADY

Margaret Thatcher (usually known as Thatcher) ruled Britain throughout the Eighties and was known to her friends as The Iron Lady. According to the Guiness Book of Records Thatcher was the most powerful woman in the world and thus could bench-press all forty-three American Presidents. Ironically, however, she was not the First Lady.

---

\* the well-known actor and astronaut

Thatcher was very fit and loved to climb up International Summits with her two best friends Ronald Reagan (no relation of McDonald's) and Gorby (who she claimed was a surprisingly warm businessman, for a Russian).

*Thatcher and her friends en route to an International Summit*

At the Summits the three friends usually chatted about how disarming they all were, but sometimes if he was in a bad mood Reagan accused Gorbachev of not being disarming at all, but *proliferating.* This was A Bad Thing and caused International Tension.

### THE MINORS' STRIKE – NO BIG DEAL

When some Minors in Britain went on strike Thatcher showed how tough she could be. The top Minor was a young lad called Arthur Scarface, but Thatcher simply refused to talk to him until he grew up a bit and took his hands out of his pockets.

*Arthur Scarface*

Arthur and the other Minors were thus reduced to standing in 'Pick it' lines*, which was no good to anyone, least of all themselves. However, at least they were on the right side of the fence, unlike the Police and other Capitalist Pigs.

---

*There were also 'Lick it', 'Roll it' and 'Flick it' lines, mainly in the north of England.

During this time Thatcher was often heard to say that the Minors' Strike was Absolutely No Big Deal. This was true as in the end the minors got cold and hungry and went home for tea.

### THE BERLIN WALL – A BIG DEAL

Towards the end of the Eighties the Berlin Wall fell down owing to a surfeit of graffiti and head-banging by The German Youth.[*]

*The German Youth*

Up to then The German Youth had been utterly trapped in Germany, but as soon as the wall came down, he raced out of

---

[*] Jugend Klinsmann, who later prospered in the West as a footballer

the country as fast as he could in search of freedom and Western Night Clubs.

Soon after the Berlin Wall fell down, other walls all over Eastern Europe and Russia followed. This is known as the Collapse of Communism. Some people also regard it as the End of History but this is wishful thinking.

## MEMORABLE QUOTATION

Thatcher once remarked, 'There is no such thing as High Society' which turned out to be an infamous remark and greatly angered all the Lords, Ladies and Champagne Socialists in the country.

However, it paved the way for Yuppies, who were coined in the Eighties. Yuppies were Young, Upwardly Mobile Professionals and hence the exact opposite of Hippies.* They were quite flashy and frequently sported mobile phones before they had even been invented.

---

* Hippies were Ageing, Seated and Unprofessional.

Torvill and Dean were one of the highlights of National Life in the Eighties. Torvill was a great ice skater and so was Dean and thus when they skated together in the Olympics they easily won the Gold Medal. This was mainly due to an unprecedented new spinning move they had worked out called *Perfect Sixes* which appealed greatly to all the judges, even unfair ones such as the Russians (or Soviets).

*'This Lady is not for Turning'*

Once Dean asked Thatcher if she would like to try a *Perfect Six*, but she firmly replied, 'This Lady is not for turning' so he let the matter drop.

Torvill never married Dean (or vice-versa) which caused a great deal of gossip at the time.

### FALKLANDS WAR

This quite serious war occurred when the Argentinians irrationally invaded the Falklands*, an excessively British group of islands right next to their country.† The Falklands were inhabited by one of the staunchest British citizens in the world.

*The Staunchest British Citizen*

---

* known as *La Semolina* in Argentinian
† Argentina

It so happened that the Fleet was nowhere near the Falklands at the time, and may anti-sceptics claimed it would take years to reach them, by which time even the staunchest British citizen might have surrendered.

However, Thatcher launched a thousand ships, which arrived in record time and promptly chased all the Argentinians back where they had come from.* The Falkland's War was thus a glorious victory and very popular among voting types.

Sadly, the Argentinians did not accept defeat graciously and resorted to cheating in football matches and taking drugs whenever possible.

## ETHIOPIAN FAMINE

For a while in the Eighties there was a surfeit of images of starving children in Ethiopia, where a famine was on. Luckily, however, a celebrity called Bob Gelding got so bored of this that he sang a song to try to cheer up the Ethiopians. In the song he explained very clearly that Christmas should be a time of plenty and smiles of joy, and that starvation was out of the question. The song went straight to Number One in Ethiopia, and seemed to do the trick as the images soon disappeared.

---

* Argentina

## BRIXTON RIOTS

The Brixton Riots occurred when thousands of Race Relations congregated in South London and shouted at the police, who responded with clubs and beatings, thus resulting in a severe decline in Race Relations.

*Some Race Relations*

## FAIRY-TALE WEDDING

This Wedding took place when the Queen ordered* her son Prince Charles to get married to the most photographed woman in the world† in a televised Fairy-Tale Wedding.

---

* in a brief Queen's Speech
† Princess Diana

The most famous scene of the wedding took place on the balcony of St Paul's Cathedral when Charles lost control of himself and violently embraced his new bride, breaking a nearby protocol as he did so. A billion people around the world gasped, which was a new record.

*Breaking a protocol*

However, the marriage was doomed from the start, owing to the fact that Camillagate (an old girlfriend of Charles) was always hanging around the palace tempting Charles with her tampons and knickers.

### THE TIANANMEN SQUARE MASSACRE

This massacre was named after a very brave little Chinese protester called Tiananmen who stood in front of a tank and utterly refused to let it overrun him even though the tank was more than twice his size.

Sadly, however, nobody saw Tiananmen ever again after this, as he was probably massacred.

### The End of the Eighties

Everybody knew the Eighties were over when they woke up one morning to discover that they had begun to feel nostalgic about Tina Turner, The Cold War and even Duran Duran. The Nineties (Not Yet History) had thus begun.

## END OF CHAPTER TEST

**Answer all questions in the style of either a Yuppie or a citizen of the Falkland Islands.**

1) Which is a better metaphor, the Iron Curtain or the Berlin Wall? When you come to think of it, are they both metaphors?

2) First disarm the person sitting on your left, then continue with whatever you were doing before.

3) Examine the full implications of Torvill and Dean.

4) Avoid speculating wildly about any two of the following: The End of History, The German Youth, Tiananmen Square, Duran Duran.

5) Compose (by email) a withering attack on Argentina. You should mention either Margaret Thatcher or Diego Maradonna (or both).

6) Draw a graph showing how many race relations were in Britain at the following key moments: the arrival of the Windrush, the death of Gandhi, the Brixton Riots, the Ethiopian Famine.

# Chapter 9

## NOT YET HISTORY

### INTRODUCTION

Events occurring after the Eighties (even Wars and Dictators) are Not Yet History as they do not have the Benefit of Hindsight. This is necessary in order to tell the difference between True History and Passing Ephemera. Examples of Passing Ephemera are Yasser Arafat, David Cameron and most of the world's population generally.*

However, even Top Historians enjoy predicting who or what will become True History, and thus this chapter is fully within the rules even though it is not (yet) on the Syllabus.

---

*It is sometimes claimed that Passing Ephemera such as David Cameron *are* history (i.e. if their photo is not in the newspaper for three consecutive days or polls show that half of all married women would like to stroke Gordon Brown). However, this is a almost certainly just a metaphor and thus untrue.

## Thatcher Steps Down

Soon after the Eighties Thatcher was forced to step down tearfully from her Office. This was largely owing to an Unfair but Traditional tax she tried to impose on Poles.[*]

*Thatcherites*

Thatcher's power waned fast after she left her Office, and it passed to her many children, known as Thatcherites.

### Major - Something of a Misnomer

John Major was voted top Thatcherite but was something of a Misnomer from the start, revealing that he was in fact

---

[*] If she had been successful it is highly unlikely that the recent Wave of Poles would have occurred.

not Major, but *Weak*. Therefore one of his first actions was to allow himself to be torn apart somewhere over Europe. This threw his Party into disarray (as people didn't know if they were still invited).

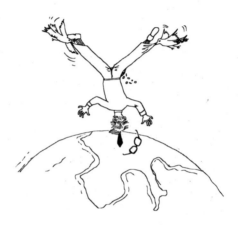

*Major: somewhere over Europe*

Major's wounds were patched up and the Party went ahead, but it was not a Success. The boys (Euroseptics) and the girls (Europhillies) hardly mingled at all, standing in opposite corners of the House and hurling insults and knives at each others' backs.

Major's absence at this event was later explained when it emerged that he had been getting Back to Basics with the Minister of Poultry Edwina 'Chicken' Currie. He romantically continued to consort with Chicken even when she was forced to resign after admitting that she had laid most of the poison eggs in the country.

*Chicken with a Poison Egg*

In the end Major weakly lost a General Election, even though he loved nothing more than the *thwack* of leather on willow and was thus highly English. Some Historians now feel a great sympathy for him, arguing that Major's weakness was not really his fault, but hereditary. However, others hold him responsible for the long-term decline of the Party in England.

# New Labour

New Labour won the election for the following reasons:—

## 1 - Tony Blah Himself

Tony Blah Himself was the first Labour Party Leader who was also an Asset. This was because he was at least five times as young-looking, good-looking, forward-looking and sideways-looking as everyone else put together, especially the Conservatives.

One of the most forward-looking things Blah did was to make Clause 4 illegal. This was an Insubordinate Clause* designed to make the Labour Party unelectable. It controversially stated that 'There must be Ownership of all Common Workers' Hands and Brains and Equitable Distribution thereof'.

The Common Workers were very relieved when Blah abolished this Clause, and thus voted for him in their Droves.†

---

\* by the Marx brothers and Engels
† white vans

*Voting in their Droves*

## 2 - MODERNISATION

Blah also changed the name of his Party from The Labour Party to New Labour. The technical word for this behaviour is Modernisation, and it is a Good but Meaningless Tactic.

By contrast, the Conservative Party[*] showed how conservative[†] it was by keeping the same name it had always had[‡]. This approach is called being Reactionary[§], and is generally regarded as a Bad Tactic[¶].

---

[*] with a big C
[†] with a small c
[‡] with a big C
[§] with a small c
[¶] with at least two small c's

## 3 - Smear Campaign

By the time of the election, most Reactionaries (e.g. David Mellors) were smeared from head to toes in a sticky substance called Sleaze, concocted in a factory at Millbank. For this reason many voters did not find them as appealing as Blah, who was unprecedentedly clean, especially at peak viewing times.

*Sleaze*

## 4 - A Landslide on Election Night

This was either a Cause or Effect (and vice-versa) of Blah's victory, and obliterated almost all the Reactionaries in the country.

### Blah Blah Blah

For the sake of convenience, New Labour should be divided into Domestic and Foreign Policies.

### The Millenium Dome

One of Blah's main Domestic policies was a Millenium Dome, the purpose of which was to trap a Giant Millenium Bug expected to devour the Nation's computers at precisely midnight on New Year's Eve. However, in an unforeseen disaster the Bug never showed up, and the Dome was thus officially (and unofficially) declared a Waste of Tax Payers' Money.

### The Minimum Wage

The Minimum Wage was Blah's only truly Socialist policy. It made it illegal for Employers to pay their workers any less than a pittance.*

### An Incomplete Policy

The Reform of the House of Lords should perhaps be confused with the Reform of the Upper House, which might (but

---

* 1 pittance = 1.67 peanuts in today's values

shouldn't) be confused with a Loft Conversion. Together, they were an Incomplete and Ill-Thought-Out Policy, and resulted in much Unwarranted Tampering with Sacred Institutions (like black rods and piers).

*Tampering with Sacred Institutions*

Proof that the Reform was Incomplete and Ill-Thought-Out:

- Not all the Lords were reformed, only those with Hereditary Diseases.
- Not all the Lords with Hereditary Diseases were reformed, only those disliked by Blair.
- Not all those disliked by Blair were reformed, only those with Hereditary Diseases.
- Repeat *Ad Infinitum* (or *Ad Nauseam*, whichever comes first).

## Scottish Devolution

Scottish Devolution is the opposite of Darwin's Evolution, and started as soon as Blah came to power. Evidence for Scottish Devolution includes the Highland Games, the Edinburgh Tattoo (c.f. the Picts), and unprecedented incidents of hairiness.[*]

*Scottish Devolution*

The Welsh were also observed to be Devolving somewhat, though not quite so fast. The main sign of Welsh Devolution is the success of their Rugby team.

---

[*] e.g. Robin Cook

Perhaps Blah's most untraditional and thus modern idea was to make killing foxes with dogs a crime. His opponents argued that they had never heard anything so absurd*, and that on the contrary it was a crime **not** to kill foxes with dogs. This is known as a controversy, and resulted, as is Traditional, in Protest Marches through London, Protest Squelches† through Parliament, and, in the end, the Government Getting its Way.

*Countryside Squelch Through Parliament*

---

* except the Old Lady who Swallowed a Bird
† i.e. in Wellington Boots

## IRAQ - BLAH'S MOST FOREIGN POLICY

Overall, the War in Iraq was Blah's most Foreign Policy, and although he swore on his wife Cherie's life that it was not Illegal, he freely confessed that he had mixed feelings about it, finding it on the one hand *Shocking* but on the other *Awesome*.

The War in Iraq is highly controversial to this day and caused two fiercely opposed fictions: The Pro-War Fiction and The Anti-War Fiction.

### THE PRO-WAR FICTION

• Saddam had Whopping Massive Destruction (WMD), enabling him to destruct Britain and America within forty-five seconds of first having the urge.

*Saddam Having the Urge*

- Even if he didn't have Whopping Massive Destruction, he was a Bad Thing, and should be destructed himself.

- However much he denied it, he was Fundamentally a Muslim and hence an intimate friend of Bin and Caliban.

- As soon as Saddam had been Destructed, Iraq would quickly turn into a green and/or pleasant land.[*]

Prime Minister Blah proved how good he was at Pro-War Fiction by writing a very sexy book. This was called *The September Dossier* and became an instant bestseller.

*A very sexy book*

---

[*] perhaps Denmark

However, some people at (especially at the BBC) felt that it was far too sexy and thus should not be broadcast before 9pm at the very earliest. Blah then made some independent Enquiries into the matter, causing the BBC to suddenly change its mind and apologise profusely.

## THE ANTI-WAR FICTION

The Anti-War Fiction was not a very good read, but should nevertheless be summarised (see below):

- Fundamentally, Muslims were a Good Thing, and thus not to be confused with Bin Laden, Al Qaeda, the Koran etc

- The War was unfair owing to American might, firepower, overwhelming force, cheeseburgers etc

- Several Iraqis were Civilians and thus did not deserve to be damaged, however collaterally.[*]

- The Real Reason for the War was to get Oil, which was the favourite foodstuff of most Americans.[†]

---

[*] accidentally on purpose
[†] with the possible exception of burgers and pancakes for breakfast

## War Fiction

As soon as the Americans rolled into Baghdad, Saddam was executed and thus instantly toppled over symbolically. (At that moment he happened to be standing very still on one leg in the main square, thereby symbolising Compression and Tyranny.)

*Americans Rolling into Baghdad*

## Wave of Jubilation

The Fall of Saddam caused a short-lived but temporary Wave of Jubilation, which ended when it was realised that Iraq sadly hadn't changed into Denmark, Holland or even France.

## A Crucial Difference

Partly owing to their previous postings in Belfast*, British troops are among of the worst-equipped and most understanding folk in the world (along with Dalais, Llamas and the better sort of shepherdess). They are thus popular.

American troops, on the other hand, are well-equipped, have never ever heard of Belfast, and are often specially trained to use violence on their enemies.† They are thus reviled.

## Inconclusive Conclusion to The Iraq War

Most politicians strongly feel that is necessary for British and American Troops to remain in Iraq until such time as it is necessary for them to withdraw. This is logical but inconclusive.

## America

For most of the Not Yet History period America was ruled by the evil Bush Dynasty‡, consisting mainly of George Senior and his ignorant yet rather dyslexic son George W.

---

* The Irish equivalent of Baghdad
† e.g. in the Korean War, Vietnam, Hiroshima etc
‡ ironically all from Dallas

When George Senior led his people into a Gulf and thus lost their good will, the highly Democratic and Sexual President Bill Clinton occupied the White House* for a short time. However he was soon caught consorting sexually with a Russian spy in his oval office. At first Bill Clinton hotly denied this, arguing on National Television that:

- Despite appearances, he had been eating pizza and not having sexual relations with that woman
- Despite appearances, the American people really should know the difference by now
- Despite appearances, his only sexual relation was his wife Hilary Clinton

*Not Sexual Relations*

---

* the American equivalent of Buckingham Palace

However, all of the above turned out to be Untrue, and Bill Clinton was thus forced out of his Office (even though he made a charismatic yet grovelling apology on National Television).

He was replaced by George Senior's son, the homespun President George W.

## ANOTHER MEMORABLE DATE

Shortly after W arrived in his Office a new Memorable Date occurred, although at first opinions differed as to what exactly it was. The British claimed it was 11/9[*], but W thought it was 9/11[†].[‡] In the end W won the argument, on account of America being Top Nation.

However, it was agreed by all that the Date is much more memorable without the year. This is known as an International Consensus, and will hopefully change History forever.

Another important fact about 9/11 is that on that day the two Top Terrorists in the world, named Al Qaida and Bin Laden,

---

[*] 11th September

[†] 9th November

[‡] c.f. similar disagreement between Linen and Trotsky about the Russian Revolution

hijacked four aeroplanes and crashed them right into America. This caused at least two towers* to collapse prematurely.

Even though they had made him excessively popular with voting types, President W did not trust Al and Bin one bit. He thus made a Histrionic Speech on National Television, claiming that they were responsible for many Axes of Evil all around the world, including in Iraq, Iran, Persia, the Gulf, the Middle East, Mesopotamia, Afghanistan, and even North Korea.

The people of North Korea and Iran had Nuclear rather than Conventional Axes, which were able to sever millions of American heads at the touch of a button. W insisted that on no account should these be allowed to get into the hands of the wrong lumberjack, but sadly this had already happened.

*Right Lumberjack*

*Wrong Lumberjack*

---

* known as The Twin Towers (c.f. Wembley Cathedral)

One of W's most famous and homespun policies was to try to *smoke out* Al and Bin from their hiding place in Afghanistan. In order to do this he ordered British and American planes to drop their homespun bombs all over the place.

This policy did not work as W ignorantly had not realised that Afghanistan was both overseas and at least twice the size of his family ranch. Al and Bin thus remained alive and well somewhere in the mountains. However, W's bombs did get rid of Caliban for a few minutes, which was a Good Thing as:

- Caliban had banned everything on the island, including Cali* and twangling instruments, which had previously been very popular.

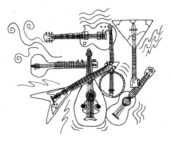

*Twangling Instruments*

---

* Arabic for bikinis

- Caliban owned lots of Conventional Axes of Evil, but fortunately was too primitive to have any Nuclear ones.

- Caliban had been on rather intimate terms with Bin.

- Caliban's Regime was unfair, as only boys had to go to school, whereas girls were allowed to stay at home and dress up in veiled costumes.

Once the smoke from W's bombs had cleared, Caliban came down the mountain to rule the island all over again.

### South Africa and Nelson Mandela

Up until the Not Yet History period South Africa had always been ruled by an Apartheid* Government, consisting largely of Boas, Klerks and other Smutty types.

At this time there were three colours of people in South Africa – Pure White people, Genuinely Black people, and Coloured† people. The Pure White people were all rich as they owned everything in the country, including all the diamonds, carrots, carats, Coloured people and Genuinely Black people.

---

\* Racist

† Orange

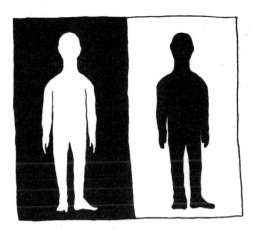

*Pure White*          *Genuinely Black*

In stark contrast, the Human Rights of the Genuinely Black people in South Africa were severely constricted under the Boas. For example they were not permitted to share a bus or even a toilet seat with a Pure White man, or play cricket except quietly among themselves in the dirt. They were also forced to live in Ashanti towns*, and frequently massacred and imprisoned (or vice-versa).

The Orange people were no better off than the Genuinely Black people. This is proved by the fact that a large area of the country was declared an *Orange Free State*.

---

* slums on the outskirts

To show how much it Officially Disapproved of all this, the International Community created a Wave of International Sporting Committees, under the leadership of Geoffrey Boycott.

This resulted in several excessively stern measures:

- The **ICC** ruled that only unofficial cricket teams would be sent to play against South Africa.
- The **IRC** ruled that only unofficial rugby teams would be sent to play against South Africa.
- The **IPPC** ruled that only unofficial ping pong teams would be sent to play against South Africa.

These tactics were dubbed Boycotting, and were a very clever way of exerting International Pressure on the South African government without unduly messing up anyone's economy.

Eventually the lack of official sports fixtures caused the Apartheid Government to collapse out of sheer boredom. Nelson Mandela* was thus released from prison, instantaneously ushering in a new era of Racist Harmony.

---

\* the Top Black Man in the world

## WAVE OF WAVES

Around this time there was a Wave of Waves.

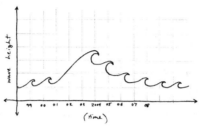

*Wave of Waves*

The first wave occurred on the stroke of midnight on New Year's Eve and was instantly known to be a *Tsunami*. This is a Japanese swear-word and is only used when the situation is very serious.

Tragically Asia was full of holiday-makers when the *Tsunami* arrived. The holiday makers were mainly visiting the place[*] to have the holiday of a lifetime, and had not at all been expecting to drown. Thus the Tsunami was ironic (as well as tragic).

Several Asians were also quite affected[†] by the *Tsunami*,

---

[*] Asia

[†] drowned

especially those who had been lying low in coastal areas. However this was not ironic as the drowned Asians were not having the time of their life when the *Tsunami* arrived. Indeed they were poor and thus probably did not even enjoy high living standards.

In the West the *Tsunami* caused a wave of compassion, even among football supporters and other thugs. Some football supporters remained silent for one or even two minutes to show how sorry they were about the *Tsunami*. This was quite controversial, as others preferred to continue chatting about the *Tsunami* and thus not waste any more of their valuable minutes.

*Wave of Compassion*

The cause of the *Tsunami* was climate change, although to say this is inaccurate and perhaps even woolly thinking.

## Hurricane Katrina

Hurricane Katrina looked like being just an ordinary little hurricane when it suddenly turned about left and tore right through the rotting underbelly of modern America.[*]

This was very embarrassing for President W, as he had been claiming that America had a very healthy underbelly. However, the rest of the world were quite pleased.

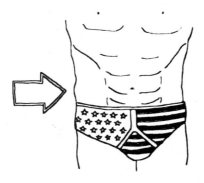

*A Very Healthy Underbelly*

---

[*] New Orleans

## The End of the Blah Era

For the last few months of his era Tony Blah became obsessed with what his Legacy would be. At first his main ideas were:

- Africa
- Bosnia
- The Middle East
- Afghanistan
- Northern Ireland
- Good Friday

However in the end it turned out that Blah's Legacy was none of the above, but Gordon Brown.


## Blah's Legacy

At first Gordon Brown hotly denied that he was Blah's Legacy, arguing that if anything it was the other way round (or vice-versa). He tried to prove this by having some very firm policies of his very own, fizz:

- almost calling an election
- almost withdrawing several troops from Iraq

However things soon went back to blah blah blah etc etc blah blah etc with nothing memorable happening until ...

2066

... when a team of British heroes defeated the Germans* in a centenary fixture at the Hastings Millenium Stadium, causing a Wave of Smugness and with luck even World War Three.

THE END

* Normans

## End of Chapter Test

**Avoid giving straight answers to any of the following questions.**

1) 'Education, Education, Education.' To what extent do you agree with these three policies?

2) Comment bitterly on the abolition of Clause 4.

3) Analyse the chain of events which culminated in John Prescott's purchase of 'two jags'.

4) Confuse and contrast Iraq, Iran, the Gulf, Mesopotamia, the Middle East, Pakistan, Afghanistan, The Taliban and (if you still have time) North Korea.

5) Was The September Dossier sexed up? (NB This is a very easy question, but may result in suicide.)

7) Is it fair to assume that there is something fishy about Gordon Brown? Why?

8) Decline to conjugate Asbo.

## About the Author

Ben Yarde-Buller divides his time equally between admitting his near-total ignorance of anything important and pretending to be well-informed. He lives (and occasionally works) in Devon.

## About the Illustrator

Sophie Duncan, being married to Ben Yarde-Buller, also lives in Devon. However, she consoles herself with the children and is rarely happier than when forced to produce hundreds of pictures at short notice because her husband has left the original versions on the train, on top of a cupboard etc.